A PROPHECY OF THE WAR

COLUMBIA UNIVERSITY PRESS
SALES AGENTS

NEW YORK
LEMCKE & BUECHNER
30–32 West 27th Street

LONDON
HUMPHREY MILFORD
Amen Corner, E.C.

SHANGHAI
EDWARD EVANS & SONS, Ltd.
30 North Szechuen Road

A PROPHECY OF THE WAR

(1913–1914)

BY
LEWIS EINSTEIN

WITH A FOREWORD BY
THEODORE ROOSEVELT

New York
COLUMBIA UNIVERSITY PRESS
1918

All rights reserved

Copyright, 1918
BY COLUMBIA UNIVERSITY PRESS

Printed from type, April, 1918

PUBLISHERS' NOTE

MR. LEWIS EINSTEIN's connection with the American diplomatic service began in 1905, when he was appointed third secretary of our embassy at Paris, and extended into the year 1916, when he served as chargé d'affaires on a special mission to Bulgaria. In the interval he served at London, Constantinople, and Peking, at the Algeciras Conference, and as Minister to Costa Rica. He is the author of "The Italian Renaissance in England," "American Foreign Policy, by a Diplomatist," "Inside Constantinople: A Diplomatist's Diary during the Dardanelles Expedition," and of numerous monographs and addresses on diplomatic, literary, and art history. The two essays in this volume formed part of a series which appeared in the *National Review* of London. The first was published in January, 1913, and the second in November, 1914. They are now republished both as records of the past and as warnings for the future.

FOREWORD

Mr. LEWIS EINSTEIN is one of the men whose work has kept alive the fine tradition of the union between American diplomacy and American letters which is illustrated by such names as those of Lowell and Motley, of John Hay and Maurice Egan. In the two chapters of this little book he gives proof of a prescience in world politics very rare among American statesmen. He foresaw the war. He foresaw our entry into the war. He sees clearly the need that our association with the British Empire shall be one of the closest friendship because it would be an unspeakable calamity for us if the British Empire succumbed to Germany; and after the war Germany will once more begin her campaign to render America the dupe and tool of European militarism by breeding hostility to England; and with this end in view she will employ everybody, from organizers of German-American Alliances to editors of German-American papers; and of course she counts in advance on the support of politicians like Senators La Follette and Stone and editors like Messrs. Hearst and Viereck.

Under such conditions it is well to have Americans like Mr. Einstein — who, like myself, is not of English blood — point out why England is now what a century ago she was not, our natural ally; and why Germany, in view of the appalling results of her sordid and brutal soul-training for the last forty years, cannot be anything but our enemy until the whole moral and political attitude of her people is fundamentally changed. The pacifists of the Norman Angell type, whether in England or America, and the silly men and silly women who listen to them, are, as they have been, the potent enemies of the peace of justice and the tools of alien militarism. Unfortunately in this country, while there has at times been a repulsive social anglo-mania among limited classes, the political danger has always been from the appeal of demagogic politicians to the anti-English vote. This manifested itself in the cautious meekness with which our governmental authorities protested against the repeated wholesale murders of our men and women by German submarines, compared with the hectoring attitude assumed towards Great Britain over mere property rights — a striking inversion of Abraham Lincoln's insistence on putting the man above the dollar. Mr. James Brown Scott, in his "Survey of International Relations between the United States and Germany," justly remarks: — "The reader experiences a shock, on turning from the German to the British correspondence, to note the cold and unyielding terms in which American rights concerning property were insisted upon. It would seem as if the American Government feared a rupture with the Imperial German Government . . . and that the Pres-

FOREWORD

ident and his advisers had determined that no act on the part of the United States, that no unguarded word or expression in correspondence with Germany, should give the Imperial Government a pretext, much less a cause, to turn against the United States if it should seem to stand in the way of the realization of the purpose (the destruction of England and the enslavement of Belgium) upon whose realization the German Government had bent its energies and upon which the German people had set their heart. . . . The neutrality which the President impressed upon his fellow countrymen was not merely the neutrality of action; it was the neutrality of thought and expression." This neutrality was neutrality between right and wrong; we persevered in it for two years and a half, and then the President, on April 2 last, announced that "the wrongs against which we now array ourselves are no common wrongs; they cut to the very roots of human life . . . Property can be paid for; the lives of peaceful and innocent people cannot be. The present German submarine warfare against commerce is a warfare against mankind," and again on August 27 last: — "the object of this war is to deliver the free peoples of the world from the menace and the actual power of a vast military establishment controlled by an irresponsible Government which, having secretly planned to dominate the world, proceeded to carry the plan out without regard either to the sacred obligations of treaty or the long-established practices and long-cherished principles of international action and honor . . . which stopped at no barrier either of law or of mercy; which swept a whole continent within the tide of blood — not the blood of soldiers only but the blood of women and children also and of the helpless poor . . . the American people have suffered intolerable wrongs." All of this was absolutely true; and it was exactly as true when the *Lusitania* was sunk as it was two years later. It was true throughout the period of our neutrality.

Under such conditions it is well to have a conscientious and highminded American citizen, who is also a trained and able diplomat, write such a little book as this.

        THEODORE ROOSEVELT

SAGAMORE HILL,
February 3, 1918

CONTENTS

	PAGE
FOREWORD	7
THE ANGLO-GERMAN RIVALRY AND THE UNITED STATES	15
THE WAR AND AMERICAN POLICY	50

THE ANGLO-GERMAN RIVALRY AND THE UNITED STATES

AMERICAN life is still too intense, the problems of its economic development, and the relations between the individual and the State, still, too, unsettled, to have aroused an interest in the nation at large in questions of foreign policy which are no less far-reaching in their nature because not visibly oppressive. Yet the recent vast extension in foreign trade, and the gradual industrial evolution of the country, coupled with the growth of population, causing American exports to be increasingly manufactures, and decreasingly agricultural, must inevitably bring about an augmenting attention to questions of external order. Already, within the last decade, this has become noticeable in the importance which the so-called "Open Door," in China, and the relations with Latin-America have assumed before the public eye. In both instances trade, present and future, has been the foundation and the objective of interest. The political cloak assumed, in the one case, by often repeated formulas regarding the integrity of China, in the other, by the Monroe Doctrine and American sisterhood, has covered the very legitimate self-interest presented by the extension of commercial relations and the growth of the nation's influence.

Beyond this, however, watchfulness ceased. The affairs of Europe, picturesque and weighty as they appeared, yet seemed to have no direct visible relation to the United States. In whatever direction might lie natural sympathies, the country as a whole remained unaware that its own interests were in any way concerned or affected by the future of the European problem, and continued indifferent thereto. A traditional disinterestedness continued as potent a formula of statecraft as half a century ago, without Americans realizing

A PROPHECY OF THE WAR

that altered conditions rendered necessary a modification of this attitude, and that the vast extension of international interests and the complexity of modern life no longer permitted former isolation. While the country had consciously altered its political, strategical, and economic situation in the world by the creation of new oversea interests and the industrial growth of a century, it yet cherished the illusion of being able to preserve intact diplomatic ideas that had long since served their time. The belief is still diffused that since in Europe America had no territorial interests nor ambition, it had likewise no solicitude and could with impunity remain indifferent to whatever occurred on its political plane.

A brief retrospect suggests, however, ample proof to the contrary. The European balance of power has been such a permanent factor since the birth of the republic that Americans have never realized how its absence would have affected their political status. American national existence was brought about by European dissension. When Pitt resisted Napoleon, the justifiable irritation we felt against British high-handedness at sea caused us to forget that England's fight was in reality ours as well, and that the undisputed master of Europe would not have been long in finding pretexts to reacquire the Louisiana territory which, except for England, he would never have relinquished. When the Holy Alliance endeavored to concentrate the power of Europe under the banner of legitimacy and divine right, Canning, by inspiring the Monroe Doctrine, interposed an effective restraint in the Western Hemisphere, and in the oft-quoted phrase, "called in the New World to redress the balance of the Old."

Fifty years later, had England joined France in recognizing the Confederacy or in her abortive Mexican adventure, the history of the United States might have run a different course. At no time since the foundation of the Republic could a change materially altering the ancient European balance of power have been brought about without perceptibly affecting American interests and the position of the United States. Even to-day, in spite of the enormous increase in the country's resources and population, this political axiom holds as true as it did in the period of national formation and weakness. The undisputed paramountcy of any nation, both by land and sea, must inevitably make that Power a menace and a peril to every other country. In the words of a distinguished Secretary of State, Mr. Olney, were the career of a Napoleon ever again to approach or even to threaten repetition, not merely sentiment and sympathy, but the strongest consideration of self-preservation and self-defense might compel the United States to take sides. It may therefore be of interest to survey the forces of war and peace to-day at work in Europe and see if there lies any menace to that balance of power, the preservation of which is essential to its national security.

At a time when arbitration and peace movements have assumed an unprecedented importance, it is a curious commentary on the age that there should likewise be so vast an increase of armaments and military preparation. The same skepticism in abstract justice, the same belief in the possible imminence of a great conflict, the same desire on the part of every nation to be the arbiter of its own political fortunes, is apparent throughout the world. A feeling of unrest, moreover, has spread over Europe, and the inflammable state of its public opinion is everywhere noticeable. The modern conception of the nation in arms, and the prolonged situation of a peace constantly more prepared for war is not the only cause for the existence of this spirit. The fresh taxation imposed by economically wasteful armaments, at the same time as nations find themselves increasingly compelled to embark on extensive and expensive programs of social reform, have contributed to augment the cost of life and the consequent dissatisfaction. There is, moreover, a growing discontent throughout Europe with the system of parliamentarism and certain effects of representative Government. France, England, and Germany are all experiencing this, though for different causes and with different purposes in view. To a nation confronted by internal difficulties the diversion of an energetic foreign policy appealing to a united patriotism is always a possible alternative. That it has rarely been abused stands to the credit of European statesmanship. But in any survey of the existing situation it lurks in the background as a dangerous possibility.

It remains an anomaly that modern democratic government has been no more peaceful than former absolutism. Moltke's prophecy that popular rule enhanced the likelihood of war was correct. The situation lately witnessed in the parliamentary discussion over the Moroccan agreement in both Germany and France, where the leaders of political parties were far more combative and unyielding than their Government, proved significant, though in the one instance hostility was directed against England, while in the other it was against the compromising attitude on the part of the French Government. The high sensitiveness of a proud people, the confidence in its own strength, and the critical and often malignant scrutiny to which every Government is now exposed from within, are all factors contributing to embitter the atmosphere of international relations by stiffening the attitude of those in power.

Various elements have thus contributed to bring about the present state of restlessness and uncertainty in Europe. Nor are other signs wanting to confirm this. Like the flight of birds before a storm, some indication of the belief in the likelihood of an impending conflict may be gathered from the recent efforts on the part of the smaller European States to preserve their neutrality and their independence in the event of the

A PROPHECY OF THE WAR

greater Powers going to war. Belgium, Holland, the Scandinavian countries, and Switzerland, have each quite recently taken stock of their position in such event, and embarked on fresh military or naval programs to increase the national security. A wave of renewed militarism and nationalism has spread over Europe. France, where it had lain dormant for years, is now witnessing an intense revival provoked by the recent difficulties with Germany over Morocco, and excited by its splendid success in aviation. In Russia the painful awakening after the Manchurian War has led to a reorganized army and the construction of a new navy. In Austria-Hungary the difficulties attending the late annexation prompted a military reform, while gratitude to Germany for the assistance rendered during that crisis, has led to an extensive battleship program and awakened for the first time naval ambition. Even Italy, whatever be the future of her newly designed African Empire, realizes that she has condemned herself during many years to come to a vastly increased expenditure for armaments.

The sources of European unrest could, however, be lightly dismissed without the antagonism between Great Britain and Germany. In spite of the attempts made on both sides to explain it away, and to dwell on the pacific disposition animating the construction of new "Dreadnoughts," this remains as an irreducible fact obscuring the political horizon. Nor should it be regarded as a mere contest for commercial supremacy on the part of two countries, one seeking to preserve, the other to gain new markets. Intelligent Germans are the first to recognize that neither their merchants nor their trade suffer in British colonies. Beneath it lies the deeply conscious rival ambition of two great nations, the one to maintain undiminished the heritage conquered by its forebears, the other to obtain the place "under the sun" which it regards as its right. And the magnitude of this issue is enhanced by the hardly lesser constellations

A PROPHECY OF THE WAR

gravitating around the rivals, each with its own historic traditions and interests, but who have realized comparative security in a system which finds its political expression in the series of alliances and understandings forming the balance of modern Europe.

Paradoxical as it may seem, the grave danger of the present relations between Great Britain and Germany lies in the fact that there is no real difficulty between the two Powers. Where a concrete obstacle stands in the way, by compromise and mutual goodwill it may be removed. In recent years the Anglo-French and Anglo-Russian negotiations, by a judicious policy of give-and-take, smoothed out through diplomatic means the colonial rivalry of a century. But between Germany and England similar adjustment is impossible. Their antagonism presents nothing concrete save rival ambition. Both Powers are logical and right in their attitude. From England's point of view she is carrying out her traditional policy of wellnigh four centuries. Whether set forth by an Elizabethan Cecil or a modern Lloyd George, whether directed against a Spanish Armada, the ambition of Louis XIV, the legions of Napoleon, or the might of William II, the purpose is the same. The same causes have made her the enemy of France and Russia and the friend of Prussia, which make her to-day the friend of Russia and France and the adversary of a united Germany seeking oversea expansion.

The position of Germany is no less logical. Having achieved her unity and imperial position by blood and iron, there is no reason why she should abandon the element of armed force which has been the mainspring of her triumph. Patriotic Germans may differ among themselves whether an increased naval program is advisable, but the nation is practically united with regard to the importance of maintaining her military supremacy, both by reason of her exposed central continental position and because of the unhealed wound inflicted on her Western neighbor. It is no fault of Germany if her strength is so huge that Europe trembles when she moves. Nor is she to blame if in the quest for new outlets her efforts at expansion under her own flag are thwarted by the colonial empires of her rivals. The unfortunate position of Germany in this respect is readily apparent, but less obvious is any peaceful remedy compatible with the interests of neutrals. The suggestion lately advanced of compensation in the Congo, or in the Portuguese colonies, even if practicable, would only be a later cause of difficulty. It might delay, but could not arrest, the growing antagonism between two great countries in their struggle for supremacy. The appetite for colonies is fed on what it consumes, and a justifiable desire for more suitable frontiers or enlarged boundaries would be the inevitable result of such surrender. What on one side could be regarded as generosity, would on the other be interpreted as weakness, with the invitation for subsequent aggression brought about by the pressure of strength.

There is no desire herein to criticize Germany. Her action, present and prospective, is that of a great nation conscious of its force, but conscious also of the limitations of its present exercise and of having arrived too late in the field of colonial enterprise and conquest. On the side of Germany there should, however, be less irritation at the acts of other Powers desiring to preserve their own, and unwilling to diminish an Empire won by the valor and foresight of their ancestors.

While the Anglo-German antagonism finds sources of friction in Africa, its essence is, however, far more metropolitan than colonial, and its character psychological more than commercial. The feeling of hostile antagonism exists to-day among the English and German people to a greater extent than in their Governments. The latter realize vividly the terrific responsibility of such a conflict, the magnitude of the interests involved, the catastrophic nature alike of victory or defeat. In the fact that neither can wish to precipitate this contest lies the surest hope for peace.

Sir Frank Lascelles not long ago remarked that as each side awaited the other's aggression, it is likely that peace would long continue. Mutual hesitations exist which must counsel prudence. The prestige of Germany and of the Hohenzollern Dynasty, acquired by war but fortified by peace, is too great to risk everything in a struggle which if unsuccessful would shake the foundations of the throne. German military science has as its axiom, moreover, to embark on no war unless certain of success, while the destruction of its seagoing commerce is accepted as inevitable. France had in the past appeared to Germany as the hostage for England. But even in this, victory no longer seems as certain as in the past. In the eyes of experienced observers, the German army has deteriorated in recent years, while the French has commensurately improved. Now that the latter is no longer honeycombed by dissension, its still-existing superiority in artillery and its new development of aviation give it certain advantages over the greater numerical strength of Germany. For the first time, also, since Waterloo, England is able to throw a military force of consequence on continental soil. The six British divisions of professional soldiers equipped for foreign service and ready for early mobilization are to-day an actuality which Germany cannot fail to consider, and which should contribute toward remedying any inferiority in men from which France would suffer. The fields of Belgium may again witness a struggle where the descendants of Napoleon's and Wellington's men will this time stand side by side against Blücher's.

If the uncertainty of victory on land as on sea thus imposes a restraint on the German warlike spirit, the tremendous consequences of a conflict likewise speak for prudence in Great Britain. The danger of a contest which would be a matter of life and death to her, the terrific sacrifices entailed even in the event of victory, the risk of starvation at home in case of disasters at sea, the possibility of invasion, the destruction of the Empire if defeated, are all nightmares to appal the most venturesome statesman.

There is little danger that, conscious of these grave responsibilities, any German or British Government would do ought to precipitate a conflict of such gigantic proportions, however favorable the moment might appear. But there is serious danger lest, in an atmosphere as surcharged as is the present, with the deep-rooted feeling of hostility existing on both sides, some petty cause of friction, or some paltry colonial quarrel, inflaming public opinion, should induce either Government to prefer a foreign war which it might regard as inevitable to domestic humiliation. The explosion provoked by the so-called Agadir incident, which brought three nations to the verge of war for a few square miles of Moroccan sand, is indicative of the intensity of feeling aroused, and of the pregnancy of danger. Future war or peace is to-day in the hands of the English and German people far more than in that of their Governments. The decision rests with them not to goad the latter into assuming positions or advancing pretensions from which honorable retreat will have become impossible.

Whatever be the future of this situation, a farsighted statesmanship compels the United States, as it does every other nation, to take cognizance of the possibility of a conflict breaking out in the near future between Great Britain and Germany, and to consider in what manner we would be affected by it. It is an easy remedy to repeat the old adage about our proverbial noninterference in European affairs. With all respect toward a policy which in the past has been thoroughly sound, it cannot be said in this instance to offer a complete panacea. A struggle between the two nations, even though it did not set ablaze the rest of Europe, cannot leave America indifferent. In too many regions of the world would our interests be affected by its reality.

It would withal be absurd to deduce from this that we should be dragged into a war against our inclination. The alternative of arms is no necessary consequence of diplomatic interest, and in such a conflict our direct participation would, if we maintain our strength, be most unlikely. This should not, however, excuse any neglect on our part to consider the various political, strategic, and economic points of view in regions of the world interesting us, where such struggle would react upon them, or how the balance of power, which it should be our policy to preserve in Europe, would be affected by the contest. An indication of its far-reaching nature, independent of the actual field of hostilities, would, for instance, be presented in the Far East, where the even temporary withdrawal of European influence would leave us face to face with a commensurately more powerful Japan. To say nothing of the Philippines, the situation thus created depends on the degree of stability and strength attained by China. It is not difficult, however, to conceive of circumstances where to insure respect for the often pledged integrity of that State would lead us toward a course of action which we would be obliged to adopt single-handed, and without the benefit of such diplomatic support as in the past we have received from friendly Powers.

Omitting, however, from consideration the extent to which the almost inevitable conflagration would affect the world in a conflict between Great Britain and Germany, three general possibilities are open: (1) The victory of the former; (2) The reverse; (3) A war of indefinite result.

So far as we are concerned, the first alternative would be the least likely to materially alter the existing status. England might conceivably recover a pecuniary indemnity and deal a death-blow to German oversea commerce. But the German colonies are not such as to sensibly attract a conqueror, nor would a change in their title affect us in any way. While the predominant position of Germany upon the European Continent would be shattered, the balance of power would hardly be affected, even though the disposition of its weight were altered. The insular position of Great Britain debars her from continental ambitions, and any attempt to assert herself in such manner would both run counter to all her traditions and be stoutly resisted by former allied States. It is fortunate that in modern times no nation has succeeded in being paramount on both land and sea. Great Britain has hitherto refrained from unduly developing her military strength and there is no reason to anticipate that flushed by victory she would adopt a different course. Her naval superiority, which is a matter of life and death, menaces no one, though it bars the way to Germany already supreme on land. But for us it represents an essential element in the maintenance and stability of the European balance of power.

If the terms of peace after such a war were to be dictated in London, the situation as it affected us would be radically reversed. While defeat for Germany might prove disastrous to the dynasty, for Great Britain it would be fatal to the Empire, whose disintegration would almost inevitably ensue. It is apparent that the fate of Canada and the British possessions in America immediately concern us. Of Canadian loyalty to the Empire there is here no question. It is certain that, like the other self-governing British colonies, she would to the best of her ability support the mother country. But if the fortune of war prove adverse, there is no reason to suppose that Canada would long continue under the control, however nominal, of a parent State deprived of prestige and authority and ruined by an unsuccessful war.

Nor is it necessary to proceed so far. The active participation of Canada in such conflict would by its very nature invite reprisals. If after a series of disasters Great

Britain should be crushed and her fleet destroyed or captured, Canada could not by herself stand up against an all-powerful enemy, and the fate of the Crown colonies would be even more immediate. A strong appeal would in all likelihood be made for our protection, which could hardly fail to awaken generous response. The consequence of any such action on our part is apparent, reinforced, moreover, by an alternative which in contradiction to the Monroe Doctrine would ask us to countenance a transfer of sovereignty upon the American Continent for the benefit of a European Power hitherto deprived of such possession.

Without going to the length of such extreme conclusions, a third and more likely possibility would be that of a contest long drawn out between the two countries wherein neither could obtain decisive advantage. In spite of the paper proof that a lengthy war presents to-day an economic impossibility, there is no practical evidence to substantiate this theory, and there are distinguished economists who believe that the modern system of credit is peculiarly adapted to facilitate the prolongation of war. When poor countries, like Japan and Russia, have been able to maintain in the field for a considerable duration armies of almost unprecedented size, there is no reason to suppose that the pinch of poverty alone would materially hasten the conclusion of a war between England and Germany. The financial aspect of this is also likely to concern us. If the struggle should be protracted, extensive borrowing will have to be undertaken, and New York is more and more becoming one of the money markets of the world. It is probable that we will be called upon, possibly by both sides, to furnish pecuniary assistance, even though the obligations of strict neutrality are somewhat questionable on this point.

The extended duration of the war may be expected from the policy Germany would presumably adopt in attempting to tire out the vigilance of a British blockading fleet by long-continued inaction, while perhaps striking isolated blows in distant waters. The recent construction in Germany of large battle cruisers, capable of holding the seas, point to the inference that in the event of war hostilities would not remain confined to the vicinity of home ports. It would not be impossible if, as in the eighteenth century, sea-fights might again take place in American waters. The capture of one of the Lesser Antilles from the English or French might offer to the Germans both a convenient haven and a pledge for subsequent negotiations. Our own attitude in this event would be one of no little difficulty. Logically, a policy of strict neutrality should cause us to remain, if not indifferent, at least passive, but it is questionable if any American Government could long tolerate the embarrassment caused by the extended continuance of hostilities in our waters, even though it led to no more regrettable nor permanent result.

If this remains a remote though possible

contingency, it is otherwise with the effect of a great struggle upon our economic interests. As all industry in the belligerent nations would be brought to a virtual standstill, it is likely that while American manufactured exports in Europe suffered there would be a greatly increased demand for foodstuffs as well as for whatever might be of utility in the conduct of war. Such commercial losses as in Europe we should experience could be more than counterbalanced by the opportunity presented elsewhere to acquire new markets and supplant former rivals. This would give an unwonted impetus to trade. Our commerce should find before it in Latin-America, South Africa, Australia, and the Far East, new outlets and new opportunities as the consequence of such a struggle.

Without a merchant marine under our flag we would not, however, be in a position to derive adequate benefit from this situation. The export of American products would be rendered increasingly difficult by the few remaining neutral bottoms with the consequent increase in freight rates. The creation of our own merchant navy thus becomes a primary necessity, whether affected by postal subventions, direct subsidies, or the admission of foreign-built ships. The sad anomaly of the present position in this respect can hardly be overstated, and until we take steps to remedy the deficiency of existing navigation laws, all our efforts to win new markets will be severely handicapped. Pride is often the forerunner of real interest, and while it is only the former that suffers to-day by the absence of the American flag on the high seas, a European war, with its wide ramifications and consequences, would soon awaken us to realizing the shortcomings of our present policy. Under existing conditions it is not difficult to picture American factories and workmen reduced to idleness because a foreign war had brought about a virtual cessation of ocean transport.

Even more important than the creation

of an American merchant marine is that at a time of uncertainty like the present, with the future still befogged, no efforts be spared to maintain our relative naval strength. Already we have fallen from the second place which, for a decade, we had occupied, and without greater exertion are likely to sink still further in the scale. The recent decision of Congress to curtail the program of naval construction could not have been less auspiciously chosen in its moment. For us to desist from a normal development, which hardly aims to do more than replace timeworn unities when all the nations of the world, great and small, are arming, is to court a disaster and to lay us open to the consequences of such imprudence. The apostles of any one-sided disarmament at a time like the present are blindly working to expose their country to a disgraceful war or a yet more disgraceful humiliation.

In the event of a European conflagration our fleet, even if maintained at its present relative strength, might find difficulty in accomplishing its double task of preserving the *status quo* in the Far East, and enforcing the neutrality of the Caribbean, where the presence of hostilities would certainly embarrass and possibly endanger American interests. The preservation of the *Pax Americana* as a corollary to the Monroe Doctrine should be our goal at all times. We have everything to gain by the peaceful and orderly evolution of existing conditions on our hemisphere and nothing by sudden or violent changes, even where our interests do not appear to be immediately affected. Hence any attempt to make of American waters the scene of war would be extremely distasteful to our policy.

The question of neutrality of the Caribbean might even be broached by diplomatic channels in time of peace. To Great Britain and France it would in all likelihood be welcome, as ridding them of solicitude in respect to islands difficult of defense, and where their sole ambition is to maintain but not to extend. Nor could Germany, possessing no territorial interests in these seas, avow pretensions which would place her in opposition to us. An international agreement having this purpose in view would thus contribute toward guaranteeing a stability of present possession, keeping the peace in the event of a European conflict and removing the likelihood of possible future changes of title embarrassing to the strategic and political position we occupy there. The alternative of a German victory, with the acquisition of a base of operations or even of territorial advantages, close to Central America, where Germans already possess great interests, and commanding the approaches to Panama, could not leave us indifferent to the future of such a prospect.

An Anglo-German conflict would thus affect us at various points and in various ways. There is hardly a branch of our national activity, governmental or economic, which would not feel its consequences in varying degree or be concerned by its outcome. While our attitude in such contest would in the beginning be one of strict neutrality, which we would endeavor to maintain, this does not mean that a far-sighted policy might not under certain contingencies impose a different course of action. However considerable the responsibility incurred, however great the bait offered, it would not be wise statemanship to remain passive if England should by any series of disasters be crushed. Even though the immediate consequence would be to throw Canada and the British Antilles into our lap, it would leave us confronted by an Empire supreme on land and sea, and would force us to pursue a preparation of armaments which for our own preservation could not be inferior to what we might be called upon to face. Without the knowledge of the country at large, the European balance of power is a political necessity which can alone sanction the continuance of an economic development unhandicapped by the burden of extensive armaments. At no time, even unknown to us, were European politics a matter of indifference to our vital interests, but if hitherto we were impotent to alter their march, a fortunate destiny preserved the existing balance independently of us.

Seeking, as little as in the past, any selfish benefit in the Old World, even though it were possible, we have to-day a distinct and legitimate duty in the family of great nations in contributing to preserve those elements which compose the balance of power, and to which we can only be blind at our later cost. The disappearance or diminution of any one State in Europe would be a calamity to us, varying with its degree. But while the importance of such extinction might not in certain instances be sufficiently close to warrant or provoke our active intervention, this would not be true with Great Britain. The disintegration of the British Empire would be a defeat for us by the erection of a Power supreme on land and sea. A German historian of reputation, Professor Oncken, of Heidelberg, has lately, with reason, expounded the view that in

1864, in the war over the Duchies, England was unconsciously defeated. "Had Schleswig-Holstein remained Danish, the right bank of the Elbe up to the gates of Hamburg not been German territory, and the Canal from the Baltic to the North Sea an impossibility, all the conditions of Germany's maritime position would have been nonexistent." French historians have similarly traced the beginnings of their disasters in 1870 to their noninterference in the affair of the Duchies. The lesson of how a failure to act later reacts should not be lost upon us.

To consider the possible contingency of such intervention by us as tantamount to an alliance with Great Britain would be untrue. Where there is no treaty there is no alliance. We do not keep England from war nor push her toward a conflict. In the event of hostilities the assertion of our neutrality would at once be made and strictly lived up to. If Germany and England choose to indulge in the luxury of war, such is their right. However much we may lament the loss of life, it is no affair of ours even though England were defeated, so long as the general balance is preserved. But if ever decisive results are about to be registered of a nature calculated to upset what has for centuries been the recognized political fabric of Europe, we can remain indifferent thereto only at our own eventual cost. If we then neglect to observe that the interests of the nations crushed are likewise our own, we shall be guilty of political blindness which we will later rue. To guard against this danger our diplomatic rôle in Europe should be far more active than in the past. Properly understood and carried out by skillful agents, it would be one which, instead of being resented, should entitle us to the gratitude of all lovers of peace, since it would be apparent that without selfish designs of our own we aimed to preserve the rights of all.

It is mistaking the nature of diplomacy to think that this would involve us in entanglements wherein we had no concern.

But it is likewise mistaking its scope for national utility to accord by an attitude of indifferent passivity a free field to the forceful ambition of any single State. Great Britain, by upholding the European balance of power, has contributed toward our free development. If misfortune in arms await her, it would be as politically unwise as it would be ungenerous to allow her to suffer unduly. A disastrous defeat inflicted by an opponent unwilling to use moderation in his victory should invite on our part a friendly mediation which in last extremity might have to be converted into more effective measures. Hence the advisability for us of preserving our strength in such a way as ever to make our counsel welcome and our action unnecessary.

THE WAR AND AMERICAN POLICY

At the last Hague Conference, where a Congress, convened for the furtherance of peace, mainly discussed the aspects of war and the method of its declaration, a Chinese delegate excited some amusement by his inquiry of what would occur if the nation to whom such declaration was addressed did not wish to receive it.

If one thing stands out more than another in the recent catastrophe, it has been the manner in which countries earnestly desiring peace, having no interest, direct or indirect, in the question at issue, have yet, through no fault of their own, been dragged into the whirlpool. An Austrian Archduke is murdered by a Servian anarchist. In the period of silence which follows, the crime is half forgotten by the world. New events occupy it: a grave crisis threatening civil war in

Ireland; a sensational trial in France; labor troubles in Russia coinciding with the French President's visit. Suddenly reparation of the most rigorous kind is demanded, and practically accepted by Servia in the interests of peace, though her official responsibility was doubtful. But the answer is termed insincere by a Government desiring to provoke war. The structure of peace tumbles like a house of cards, and within a fortnight the Belgian countryside is charred and ravaged by invading German armies, its cities burned, and the land itself, in the words of its foremost churchman, is a pool of blood.

Certainly, it is easy to apportion blame, and to indicate causes. But the superficial causes are not always the real, while philosophic reasons are often invoked where the explanation is far simpler. There are those, particularly in America, who have seen in the great war the dead hand of alliances, and regard it as the condemnation of a system which automatically extends warfare instead of localizing it. But Belgium, whose neutrality by a final touch of irony had been guaranteed by the very Power violating it, was free from all such entanglements. With alliances it is as with armaments: the example forces emulation. In addition to the gospel of force which Bismarck left as a two-edged legacy to Germany, he brought also the alliance with Austria. The Franco-Russian alliance was its inevitable reply. Yet, without the dictates of self-preservation, the formal terms of such treaties would prove of slight consequence. Italy, a member of the Triple Alliance, had no compunction in refusing to participate in what she regarded a war of aggression, while England, though free from all obligations, felt otherwise.

Yet England was as pacific as Belgium. Lord Beaconsfield once remarked that though a British Prime Minister has many interests, none are greater than the preservation of peace. At the risk of reiterating the obvious, a great commercial nation like England, with no continental ambitions, amply satisfied with existing responsibilities which she does not seek to extend, has nothing to gain by war, which, in the event of non-success, threatens her national existence. During the recent crisis no country did more for the preservation of peace. To an impartial mind, the British Blue Book is here conclusive. Sir Edward Grey's offer that if Germany would put forward any reasonable proposal, making it clear that she and Austria were striving to preserve the peace of Europe against France and Russia, England would not support the latter, remained unanswered. In the medley of German Imperial and official telegrams, the text of which has in certain selected cases been published, no reply was ever made to this.

Nor was France more anxious for war. If one nation more than another has completely changed its character, and having been the firebrand of Europe, was endeavoring to settle down to the peaceful enjoyment of its prosperity, it has been France. The increasing gravitation of the Government toward social reforms, the pronounced pacifism of its dominant political parties, the sacrifices and even humiliations endured by a proud nation, were as many pledges toward the sincerity of its desire to maintain peace. Even the recent military efforts, hardly begun and still incomplete, were a tardy rejoinder to the colossal preparations which Germany had of late years been making. No great power was less desirous for war than France, none short of national suicide would have gone to greater lengths to avoid it.

It can hardly be supposed that Russia wanted war. Even if no other reason existed, the fact that, after her disastrous experiences, she was in the midst of a military and naval reorganization which could not be completed before several years, was sufficient to make peace almost imperative. In the interests of peace she had submitted to the Austrian annexation of Bosnia and Herzegovina. In the interests of peace she had submitted to seeing a Servian army deprived of the fruits of victory after its memorable march to the Adriatic. In the interests of peace she had allowed an artificial Albanian State to be created at the expense of her Slav kinsmen. She was allowing Austria to exact punishment from Servia, and herself counseled the moderation of the reply from Belgrade. But there were limits beyond which self-respect would not let her go.

The pacific dispositions of the German people have repeatedly been noticed. There is little doubt that the vast majority did not want war. With all sides thus professing their wish for peace, and advertising their labors for its preservation, what series of colossal blunders precipitated the outbreak? How came such an apparently undesired catastrophe to occur for which no nation will take the responsibility? The Germans attribute it to the Emperor's almost accidental discovery of Russia's secret mobilization. But Russia had no interest to make war, France and England had no desire, and Belgium, the first victim, was a neutralized State. The only avowedly designed war was against Servia, which in the Austrian intention was to be a punitive expedition. The great war itself remains anonymous. Is its guilt undiscoverable?

The German people did not want war. But in a nation where, in spite of its high boast of civilization, public opinion is notoriously in its infancy, the pacific inclination of the people exercised no influence on the German Emperor and his military advisers, who regarded the moment as singularly opportune for a conflict. The famous German theory of a preventive war intended to forestall an ulterior danger found here its exemplification. The people were told they were being attacked; partial truths, denatured from their real significance, were announced to them. And the people believed the official equivocations, with the same spirit of submissive obedience with which they took up arms. If the suppleness of the Bismarck tradition had been cast aside, at least its gross misrepresentation of facts had been preserved.

A transcendental reason has been advanced by the German side, where the struggle is declared as one between Teutonism and Slavism, supported by its Western allies. The cause of war lay in the supposed designs to Servia to make herself a great Power at the expense of Austro-Hungary. Ground may have existed for such suspicion. The recent successes of Servia had strengthened the magnet of attraction for the millions of Slavs within the Austrian Empire, ill-satisfied by their treatment at the hands of a bureaucratic administration wanting in sympathy and suppleness. The tension between the two countries had further imposed on Austria repeated and expensive mobilizations on her frontiers, and a state of watchfulness conducive to irritability and harshness. From the Austrian point of view the situation was one which could not be prolonged, and the time seemed ripe. Servia was temporarily exhausted by the three wars she had been obliged to wage almost within a year, and which, if they left her victorious, had none the less crippled her. Russia, imperfectly prepared, could in turn, it was thought, expect little aid from her Western ally. Is it to be supposed that Austria wanted to fight Russia? Certainly, if she could have achieved her aim to crush Servian independence without such war, she would have preferred it. But she took the risk with full knowledge that war might, and probably would, ensue. "The remotest possible consequences of this action have been carefully considered," appeared in a Viennese official organ. The war with Servia was provoked in all deliberation. The war with Russia was accepted with full prior knowledge of its likelihood.

To what extent was Germany responsible for this? Before taking the final step it is known that Austria had consulted her and received full assent. Whether the German Foreign Office had previously read the text of the Austrian note to Servia is immaterial. With diplomatic casuistry it had probably been submitted privately, but not officially, to the German Emperor's approval. A complete indorsement was, in any case, given for a reason frankly explained by the German White Book. The fear expressed at Berlin lay not only in an eventual Servian success, but also lest the numerically preponderant Slav element within the Austrian Empire should increase at the expense of the German, and thus alter its political complexion. It seemed vital to check this movement at any cost, and preserve the Germanic influence. The war was thus made to assume the appearance of a great racial conflict which was to mark the definite victory, or defeat, of Teutonism. The criminal plot of two Emperors, seizing a supposedly favorable moment to set Europe ablaze, was dignified into a struggle of race protection, and acclaimed by two nations conscious that all military preparations had been completed while its adversaries were still unready, and believing implicitly in the victory of its armies.

Respect for treaties as "scraps of paper,"

or the rights of neutrals, or indeed respect for its own word, all disappeared in the German mind before the law of alleged necessity. The Fatherland attacked by the Slavs, the national danger and the final triumph, were visions alternately flashed by a disciplined press. Ably, if unscrupulously exploited, this has filled the German armies with a profound conviction in the justice of their cause. The wave of military barbarism sweeping over a country once civilized, is interpreted in Germany as a lofty ideal of civilization and humanity. Having identified themselves with whatever is noblest, they regard the German cause as inseparably connected therewith, and disparage their Western foes as a soulless, heterogeneous lot, prompted by jealous motives to assist the Slav barbarian.

It is well to realize the German point of view, since it explains much that is otherwise incomprehensible, and serves as a future lesson for others than the belligerents. France is thus a nation in decay, whose historical mission being over, occupies a place to which she is no longer entitled. Germany is destined to take her place. But the chief indignation has been against England, who, out of motives of jealousy, has betrayed the interests of the Teutonic race by her unholy alliance with Russia and Japan.

The neutral observer is less impressed by the insolence of the Pan-German ideal which of late years has been fostered by hysterical professors and retired officers, than by its hold upon a nation priding itself on morality, yet throwing to the winds the most elemental considerations of national honesty in the effort to win. This absence of all political scruple, coupled with a perfection of organization, a spirit of obedience and the possession of whatever resources science can procure, and accompanied by a readiness of sacrifice admirable in another cause, has made the German nation the most powerful organization for enforcing executive policy the world has yet seen. It also makes the consequences of German victory certain to extend far beyond the nations defeated.

In Italy this danger has already been understood, especially by the Socialists, who, in spite of the efforts made by their political brethren in Germany and Austria to win them over, after stigmatizing the war as one of aggression by these two countries, have realized that their success would imply a triumph of militarism, menacing Italian democracy. The fear of such victory, tending at its best to reduce Italy to the position of a vassal state, is widely spread, and in the light of German ambitions can be regarded as neither unjustified nor exaggerated. While proclaiming neutrality, the Italian Socialists have had no hesitation in expressing their sympathy for the Allies, in which they reflect the opinion of the country at large.

The consequences of German victory will not, however, be confined to the Continent of Europe. It would be casting on Pan-German ambition a willful slur to assess its aspirations so low. In the event of their success we, too, will be privileged to encounter these.

In the United States we have gazed upon the distant spectacle of war with the keen interest which the greatest event of modern times has warranted. Even as spectators, we have been thrilled by the deeds of heroism, while its train of misery and suffering has awakened our sympathy. We have relieved the plight of our stranded travelers and have watched conscientiously over the obligations of neutrality. We have scanned the situation from its commercial possibilities, and reawakened to the need of a merchant marine. We have studied the crisis from every point save one, though it is the one which most closely touches our interests. In what way will this war affect our future? Surely no graver question has ever loomed on the horizon of American policy.

For ourselves we have hitherto felt little anxiety. There has almost been a smug satisfaction at the three thousand miles of ocean separating America from the main seat of war, coupled with the feeling that we are privileged in being able to lead our life independently of the bloody childishness which has arrested the development of our commercial rivals. While such ideas may not reflect the finer instincts in the country, the consequences of the great struggle have otherwise hardly impressed themselves. The "plague on both your houses" has been a more frequent point of view than the realization of future possibilities in so far as the success of one or the other side may affect our position.

The entire military fabric of continental Europe has been one so alien to our habits of thought, and until lately to our general knowledge, that the conception of the nation in arms, which has for its basis the execution of policy, yet seemed by an odd paradox devoid of all practical wisdom. To the average American it was always a riddle why countries whose high technical skill in other directions we had frequent occasion to appreciate, should yet pay such attention to armaments. There seemed something almost childish connected with this idea which Civil War traditions confirmed rather than dispelled. We remembered with pride our citizen armies raised when danger threatened, and the patriotic determination which, on either side, saw them through to victory or defeat. We had regarded them not without reason as equal to the best professional soldiers. We remembered our great leaders who had risen in the hour of need. But we were inclined to forget that two years elapsed before the Northern armies could be welded into efficient combatant bodies, and that the long-protracted situation was only rendered possible by the disabilities which weighed equally on either side.

Between the Civil and the Spanish War, our military efficiency sank to its lowest ebb. Even afterward, in spite of new problems and responsibilities, in spite of the precariousness of our hold in the Philippines and the burdens assumed in Latin-America, we have done little to improve it. Apart from the fleet which, in the face of German naval increase, could not long keep the second position it had temporarily attained, the army, through no fault of its own, remained inferior in numbers and organization to that of the smallest European State. The armed forces of Bulgaria and Switzerland, nations less in population than New York City, far exceed our own and indeed surpass any army which we could put into the field before probably six months of preparation.

Such military inferiority has hitherto not proved a handicap nor acted otherwise than to our advantage. The economic prosperity of the nation has been largely built up by a condition of peace which has freed us from the saddling burden of armaments. In continental Europe, in spite of every euphemistic explanation, the years passed with the colors are taxes on their youth. From such necessity we have fortunately been dispensed. But we are prone, as a result, to lay undue stress on our insular position in respect to

Europe, without realizing the factors of different order which alone have made it possible. It has been far less the distance which allowed our previous weakness than it has been the division of Europe into two camps. Unrealized by the nation at large, the famous balance of power which for centuries has been the basis of European diplomacy, allowed us a freedom from military burdens which we were inclined to ascribe exclusively to our pacifism, our superior wisdom, and our favorable geographical position.

Although lately the Old World has regarded our policy toward Mexico as insolent, it yet confined itself to mere criticism as a result of the intense strain of a situation which allowed no European State to divert any portion of its strength in a secondary enterprise. We have been pleased to consider the consequence as a tribute to our high moral service rather than to the circumstances permitting us to do what we liked, where we liked, and how we liked, with our southern neighbors. So long as a European balance of power continues as before, such liberty will continue to be ours to use or to abuse. But if, as the result of this war, the predominance of one Power is asserted, our own future sphere of action, nay, our own future security, will require for its preservation steps of entirely different order.

War is so inseparable from the realities of forces, that since the issues of the struggle must depend on the success of arms, it may seem waste of time to discuss, at this stage, the premises of peace. Though convictions now take the place of knowledge, yet certain factors seem assured. By whatever paths the highroad of peace be approached, the latter can come only through the United States.

This is far from meaning that the well-intentioned efforts at mediation suggested in the atmosphere of Washington will prove efficacious before the moment is ripe. The questions at issue are so gigantic, the destiny of nations so deeply implicated, as hardly to encourage the success of any venture before the complete exhaustion of either, or of both sides — the fate awaiting the conquered is too oppressive to dispense the nations at war from anything short of their highest effort. The lately published treaty between France, Great Britain, and Russia, moreover, precludes any individual negotiation for peace. Between Austria and Germany the terms of alliance stipulate a similar arrangement, hence all hope is vain that any one nation's exhaustion might induce it to sue separately for peace. If present prospects point to the war being fought out to the bitterest end, this in no way lessons the peace-bearer's efforts. The colossal strain on the moral and material resources of every nation, the waste of blood and treasure, the increasing hardships and misery, which must be felt by those who stay at home, will all exert their silent pressure. That the wish for peace will be heard by us is certain. It is less sure that we will know how best to utilize our efforts in our own interests and in those of civilization.

If it is intended to restrict American good offices to the simple transmission of demands and the haggling over terms, the task of mediation will manifestly not be arduous. For the offering of a neutral ground on which to conduct the negotiations, United States territory or sponsorship would be unnecessary — the Principality of Monaco might as well answer such purpose. It will be urged that the moral weight of lesser countries is inferior to our own. Confidence in public morality remains a pretty fancy in the light of recent events. With the ruins of Louvain still smoldering, is it to be supposed that a victorious Germany would be more likely to feel such restraint in the moment of triumph than when the outcome was still uncertain? Our hopes may find themselves shattered, if they rely too exclusively on moral weight. In the end it will triumph, it must triumph, but under present conditions only when it emanates from a reserve of force able to make itself felt.

Although nothing has wisely been said,

it is probable that the administration looks forward to a less modest part than the one of mere transmission of negotiations between the two sides. The task of peacemaker comports so many possibilities, and the premises of peace will be of such importance in shaping the future history of the world, that as the interests affected in the settlement will extend far beyond those of the nations at war, the action of peacemaker suggests rather an extension of the part we may hope to play than any willful restriction. Nor will it be possible to make the most of our opportunities if we delay decision on the extent given to mediation until negotiations begin. While its nature and character may be left to the shaping of events, the time to prepare for it has already begun, and any further delay or remissness in that respect is likely to be attended with serious consequences.

The fear may therefore be entertained that the desire to give present expression to an exaggerated pacifism and the reluctance to avoid any semblance of departure from complete neutrality may deprive us from taking necessary measures of precaution lest they receive an erroneous construction. In reality a distinction should be made between the attitude of the Government and the sympathies of the nation in respect to the great war. The first has properly been one of entire neutrality. Our interests remain untouched, and nothing has yet occurred of a nature to affect these. If we now watch over them with vigilance, no cause for apprehension should exist.

American sympathies, on the other hand, if the feelings of the vast majority of the nation are correctly interpreted, have been wholeheartedly with the Allies. Our moral sense has revolted before the ruthlessness of the Prussian doctrine of war, and German attempts to shift the burden of aggression have only encountered a skeptical derision. Certainly, the defeat of Germany promises a moral recasting of the world. The great Liberal wave which had swept over Europe seventy years ago receded when Bismarck introduced the era of force. The battles between Germans and Allies are far less battles between different nations than they represent the contrast between Liberalism and reaction, between the aspirations of democracy and the gospel of iron. In the presence of the great forces locked in battle our feelings cannot remain indifferent. American sympathy would be untrue to its most generous traditions if it expressed any other hope than in the success of the allied cause. The difficulty for our statecraft is to reconcile such feelings with the duties of neutrality and the wish to be of service in ending the war. But this difficulty is perhaps more apparent than real. In no way does it clash with our obligations or the guiding lines of what our policy should be.

At the moment when the maximum of military efficiency has been attained by every other power, it is presuming too much on fortune to rely on the sole persuasiveness of moral force. In doing so we restrict the scope of our utility and expect an imponderable element, which is almost the test of civilization, to achieve results of importance in a moment of barbarism and under the handicap of unfair conditions. Thus far we are only curtailing the possibilities of our own beneficent action in respect to other nations. But in a struggle with problems involving such world-embracing aspects, it is by no means inconceivable that without the exercise of vigilance our nearer interests may be seriously affected. The recasting of continental Europe may be a matter of political indifference to us, but it might not be so with the transfer of authority in other parts of the globe. Though we may welcome a New Zealand occupation of Samoa, the Japanese siege of Tsingtau is not without exciting apprehension in the light of Manchurian experiences and open-door pledges, while a German move against Martinique could not be viewed with apathy. But without speculating on different possibilities which can here be evoked, it is apparent that the political aspects of peace may concern us far more closely than we now anticipate. Nor is it unreasonable to consider a possible exchange of continental territory for colonial possessions. In the event of a draw, for instance, the cession to France of Lorraine in return for certain of the French tropical colonies, among which might be Guyana, would be, if remote, a not impossible contingency. Such transfers might not be in every event indifferent to us, and we can be hardly satisfied that our unsupported moral objections during or before the peace negotiations would provide an adequate restraint in every case. We are now traversing a crisis in the history of the world when we may pay dear for undue optimism or weakness. The devil is in arms, and the old saw that the devil must be fought with his own weapons never rang truer. While we have before us the grave duty of making heard our voices in the interests of peace, we have also that of safeguarding our interests. It is well to keep our moral persuasion in evidence. It will prove more efficacious if behind it our power is apparent.

At first glance, and independently of our sympathies, the triumph of either side might seem to lead to a result which, according to the construction given, would be either indifferent or affect us equally. But a closer analysis indicates the vast difference between the victory of the Allied Powers and that of Germany and Austria. The reason is unconsciously explained by the Germans themselves, who reproached their enemies with forming a heterogeneous collection of nations, bound together without common ideal and whose sole link of union is provided by a mutual antagonism. The fairness is questionable of disparaging their enemies' motives, but it would be difficult to find three nations wider apart than France, Great Britain, and Russia. Yet the two Western States present points of contact. Both are liberal nations in the sense that they are governed by the people, and that both at the outbreak of the war were engaged in working out great programs of democratic reform. Both were satisfied with their situation as capitalist nations and had lost the appetite for conquest. In both, too, a large and influential party actively planning to bring about disarmament had only been restrained by the fear of its one-sided nature. Both, too, were Powers with American possessions whose status in the event of the defeat of their home countries would raise up new problems. Although it is likely that Germany would willingly have given us assurances in this respect or even in accordance with her record of generosity for territories other than her own, have offered us as many of the West Indies as we signified our wish to obtain, the advantage of such acquisitions might, under the circumstances, be doubtful.

With regard to Russia the situation was somewhat different, though the Russia of to-morrow is little likely to be that of yesterday. The country is now traversed by vast democratic currents whose influence must be felt more and more. The Russian specter of reaction had long tempted terrified Liberal Europe, and the nightmare was successfully utilized by Germany to bring her Socialists into line. In the Prussian War of Liberation a century ago, she had been glad enough to obtain the aid of the Cossacks, and the Russian alliance was long the goal of Bismarckian diplomacy, but she now denounced her Eastern neighbor as barbarous. It was even hoped at Berlin and Vienna that the fact of the war being primarily against Russia might keep France from living up to terms of an alliance never popular with the working classes, and maintain England neutral. But the Russian bogy of the past appeared less threatening than the German peril of the present.

The criticism leveled at the Allies had at least this foundation, that their victory meant the triumph of a combination without other than temporary unity brought about by the common wish to resist German aggression and predominance. Its success would therefore not materially affect our position. While there might be changes in the map of Europe, the rights of neutrals would be vindicated, the balance of power restored, and a relative, if not a general disarmament, most welcome to us would probably ensue. There is certainly nothing in the record of either Great Britain or France in recent years to lead any reasonable person to suppose that their efforts would in case of victory be directed against us, or would not insure a lasting peace.

Can the same be said of Germany? Without going so far as to admit the successful invasion of Great Britain, except after another war, it is not impossible to conceive the reality of the Pan-German dream, — to picture Holland, Belgium, and Northeastern France as German provinces; to see the rest of France, Italy, and Spain reduced to the proportions of vassal states, with Russia crushed, her Baltic provinces annexed to Prussia, and Poland forming part of an Austria even more completely dominated by Berlin; the Levant would be controlled through her Turkish satellite, while the possession of the French and Dutch colonies would make German influence paramount in the Far East, and in rivalry with our own through Latin-America. All this may appear to us indifferent: certainly Germany in victory, perhaps more than in defeat, will aim to flatter our opinion and enlist those sympathies which always go to the conqueror. The same German Press Bureau will extend its propaganda, and the same official instructions which caused American flags to be spontaneously waved before our departing tourists will redouble their ordered amiabilities. Though success exceed all German expectations, we still will find ourselves courted, our sagacity praised, our money borrowed until — until the ruins of the war will have made way for new edifices, the gaps in the army filled, the navy rebuilt, the fortresses and arsenals extended, the treasure replenished, and the same patient labor which lifted the Germany of 1870 to the Germany of 1914 has been repeated.

Is this the future to which we must look forward, and is the doctrine of force to be the inevitable accompaniment of progress? Yes and no. The success of modern Germany has been due to its wonderful spirit of disciplined effort in conjunction with high technical efficiency. It has not sought to conquer hearts nor to awaken sympathies. There are millions of Germans, other than Poles and Alsatians and Danes, ill satisfied with their government. The rifts of classes lie deep, with little mutual sympathy to bridge them over. The vigorous remains of Prussian feudalism, all powerful in the army and the administration, have not unfrequently clashed with the democratic aspirations of a new industrial Germany. In the stress of war the sense of discipline, the feeling of danger, and the mendacious presentation of the case have for the time fused the entire population. All parties are now on their mettle, the military aristocracy to maintain its supremacy by qualities of leadership, and the new democracy to prove its patriotism. But for those who look beyond and see peace after the great war, the entire shaping of the German future must depend on the issue. Should she be defeated, it is inconceivable that the anomalous condition under which she has retained a "Samurai" class will not terminate. No unsuccessful adventure could authorize the preservation of a military caste unable to accomplish the purpose of its existence. The new industrial Germany, representing the same Liberal elements as came to the fore in 1848, the German democracy, sincerely peace-loving, would then assert its own, and refuse to accept any longer the inferiority to which they have been relegated by a reactionary Prussian *Junkerdom*. Without wishing the destruction of the German Empire, it is possible to conceive of a new German régime, republican or monarchical, where an enlightened public opinion breathed nobler aspirations than the crude imperialism and worship of force of the present Hohenzollerns.

A victorious Germany would, on the other

hand, provide a definite consecration for the existing pyramid with its dominating military apex. It would inevitably encourage German faith in their actual institutions and incite the spirit of intolerant aggression which now spurs them on to world domination: alone of all national anthems the *Deutschland über Alles* proclaims German superiority over all the world. The instruments of Pan-German propaganda through its different leagues would once more furrow opinion and instill in it new seeds of hatred against whoever dared thwart the Chosen of the Lord. Irritability would again be manifested at any remaining relics of independence elsewhere, and reliance on the army of five million bayonets would once more be invoked on every occasion. Forecasts are hazardous, but from Germany's past record, again confirmed by success, it is obvious that the same all-prevailing spirit of militarism will maintain its ascendancy. The only difference will be, that as former elements of restraint shall have been destroyed or cowed by

German victories, an even more emphatic assertion of aggressive policy is to be expected.

With such a prospect would it be possible for a nation as alert and as intelligent as our own to continue unarmed in the future as in the past, relying solely on the peacefulness of our intentions? Grave fear exists lest, with the profound pacifism of the country, with our confidence in the vast extent of our resources, and in the patriotism of our people, we may be disposed to neglect our defenses, taking at their word German professions of friendship. Imbued with the virtue of our policies, we persuade ourselves that what is self-evident to us is also so to others. General von Bernhardi, in his book on *Germany and the next War*, alludes ironically to our childlike self-consciousness, with which we appear to believe that public opinion must represent the view which American plutocrats think most profitable to themselves. We do not realize that Germans feel equally convinced of their righteousness. But between their policy and our own the difference is that theirs never exceeds the limitations of an executive able to enforce the same; while with us a frequently incompetent diplomacy, recruited and directed rather with a view to political benefits than to larger national objectives, runs the risk of clashing with a powerful and ambitious nation able at all times to rely on the support of its armed strength.

If we do not neglect our duty, we must realize that the German triumph cannot but impose on us a military strain which in the interests of self-preservation will have to be as intense as possible. In one form or another the universal service idea will be introduced. If we are convinced of the danger of this impending curse of militarism, our existing neutrality, however sincere, cannot be disinterested with respect to a struggle whose effects on us would vary so greatly. It is well to appreciate this at a point where the issue still remains doubtful. As in the conduct of military operations, a prudent commander maintains his strategic reserve, so we may wisely employ our resources and our influence as a diplomatic reserve, and though preserving neutrality escape the ordeal of war, and at the same time reduce the likelihood of future unwelcome obligations and danger. We are able to do so in a manner easier than is commonly realized. If we wish at least to avoid partially the burdens of militarism, it is evident that we must always keep another Power between Germany and ourselves. For obvious reasons [1] that Power can only be England. In a rough way the calculation of what this would mean to us is simple to make, and may even be mathematically expressed. Just as England has wisely treated France as her "glacis," and by present assistance is defending her own future, so is Great Britain our bulwark against any foreign foe. For the purposes of security our strength in respect to Germany would have to be equal to the difference

[1] See the writer's *American Foreign Policy*, by a Diplomatist. Houghton Mifflin, Boston, 1909.

between English and German strength. The more Great Britain is crushed, the more her resources are reduced and her strategic position weakened, the greater will be the effort we shall be called upon to make.

To guard against this danger, a new conception of our diplomatic policy, or rather an extension of an ancient policy, becomes necessary. We must extend the Monroe Doctrine to England and embrace within its scope the foremost American Power after our own. It must, above all, be made plain that this is done not on grounds of common civilization or race, or tongue, but on grounds of solid interest reinforced by the weight of tradition and sentiment, but not guided thereby. In the presence of a new European danger the integrity of Great Britain has become for us a matter of vital concern. Such conception may astonish by its novelty. It will doubtless be denounced or held in derision by those wiseacres whose vision of the imperial eagle remains blurred by stagnant memories. The weight of our own traditions would seem to conspire against it. But neither our traditions nor our past experience have ever contemplated such a possibility as is now before the world. In the presence of new conditions, new ideas become necessary, and we would do well to borrow a leaf from that German realism which gauges a situation in the cold light of fact without being deviated by other considerations. We should then be able to understand the situation which a German triumph would threaten — of a nation exalted by successful war, imbued with the doctrine of force, persuaded of the destiny impelling it onward to world domination.

If hitherto we have had occasion to complain of a Germany athwart our path in the Philippines, insidiously threatening us in Latin-America, how much more will we have cause to complain when the same restraints as before no more exist; we will see her challenging our policies and chafe at her activity crossing our own, while she will declare the same of us and instill in her people the conviction that we are the enemy. The same campaign of specious education which the doctrine of a Treitschke, a Bernhardi, or a Lamprecht have planted in the German mind, persuading it of its superiority resting on force, will at the seasonable time be invoked against us. Outwardly an Emperor will proclaim his love of peace and his regard for the United States. But below, those who listen will hear the rumblings of a revived German agitation against the Monroe Doctrine, which Bismarck once described as an impertinence. Almost unsuspected by us a campaign will be going on, to contrast the lofty purpose of German idealism with the grossness of our materialism. Public opinion will once more be ably exploited to prove the superiority of German culture and the moral duty imposed upon a noble race to put an end to the dollar barbarism of America and impress upon us the superior stamp of Teutonic civilization.

If the purpose of our neutrality will have been to give Germany time to recover for her next war, if as its result England shall have been reduced to a third-rate State, the price to pay for such obedience to past traditions may come too high. Though our statesmanship be praised for its prudence, though the peaceful intentions of the German people be dinned into our ears, some day when, perhaps, the fate of Louvain has overtaken Boston, when New York will be held up to the ransom of a thousand million dollars, when improved Zeppelins will have carried, far and wide, proofs of the superiority of Teutonic civilization, there may be those who will regret the sagacity of our traditionalism.

Yet, if correctly understood, our present duty is neither arduous nor hazardous. We are averse to war, we seek no selfish benefits. We believe that by force of circumstances, when the moment for peace arrives, we, and we alone, will be able to assist the difficult progress of negotiations. This is the obvious aspect of our duty which has impressed itself on every one. Beyond it there exists, however, a perspective of national insurance in no way irreconcilable with it, though bidding us take precautions. It urges us, in order to make heard our voice and speak with the authority incumbent on our position as a great Power, to concentrate our resources and instruments of action. These are of two kinds, financial and military — neither can be neglected.

We have been somewhat inclined to disparage the association between finance and diplomacy. The nation at large was never properly enlightened with regard to its utility in China and in Central America, and not unnaturally criticized severely the employment of methods which, if sound in their basis and goal, were yet not always happily inspired and liable to misconstruction. Yet it is beyond dispute that in our banking resources, especially at a moment like the present, we possess a reserve of strength and a diplomatic leverage of great magnitude. The question is if this is to be dissipated in isolated ventures according to the affiliations or sympathies of those who control it, and who in the absence of restraining influences might consider themselves justified in following such paths as best suit their inclinations, or to be treated from a national point of view. The banking interests are as patriotic as any other, and were the feeling of their collective responsibility impressed upon them, there is every reason to anticipate that they would justify such confidence. The recent declarations of Mr. Lloyd George, that while the first hundred millions will be as easily raised in every country, the pinch will come over the last ten, may find supplementary application in our ability to advance funds. If we now hold ourselves in reserve it is likely that when the time comes, our bankers' action, if properly directed, will prove of enormous importance as an incentive to peace and a protection to our policies.

Beyond this it behooves us to dismiss once for all such ideas as have caused the fleet to be disseminated in quest of tourists, whose welfare could be looked after by other vessels, or suggest its employment for commercial uses. At a time like this there is only one use for it, namely, insurance against war. It should unquestionably be concentrated and placed on war footing. To diminish in any way almost the only real asset of active strength we possess is little short of criminal. The President, too, should call for a quarter of a million volunteers for purposes of instruction. Our existing military inferiority demands this step which menaces no one. It offers no incentive to war, but would be only the natural precaution which every other nation, great or small, whose interests can be affected, has taken. It could in no way interfere with our neutrality, but would enable our diplomacy to speak, when the moment came, with an authority which it now lacks. If the meaning of our intentions were manifest, in the event of the victory of a nation which only listens to force, our advice, if tendered at the right time, might exercise a beneficial effect. A quarter of a million raw volunteers seem little in comparison with the five millions of trained soldiers Germany has called to arms, but as an earnest of the future they would not be without significance and might save us untold sacrifices in years to come.

With German success upon the Continent of Europe we could not expect to interfere. Keen as would be our regret at the crushing of France, or the destruction of Belgian independence, we are unable to prevent either misfortune. With regard to England it is otherwise. A warning served on Germany, exhausted even though successful in war, should be adequate to restrain her from further attack upon a nation whose integral preservation after the destruction of other forces would alone separate us from a world-conquering power. The friendly visit of our fleet to British waters might provide another hint. Beyond that it should not now be necessary to go. The Monroe Doctrine would have been extended to Great Britain.

Bei Fragen zur Produktsicherheit wenden Sie sich bitte an:
If you have any questions regarding product safety,
please contact:

Walter de Gruyter GmbH
Genthiner Straße 13
10785 Berlin
productsafety@degruyterbrill.com